Bubblegum
The Groovy Guide

Bubblegum

The Groovy Guide

An essential *Bubblegum* guide

Ged Backland and Phil Renshaw

■SCHOLASTIC

The Big Ta goes out to Jez Spencer, Ben Whittington, Steph and Robert at Scholastic, Keith Auty and everyone at Carlton Cards.

Scholastic Children's Books
Commonwealth House, 1-19 New Oxford Street
London WC1A 1NU
a division of Scholastic Ltd
London - New York - Toronto - Sydney - Auckland
Mexico City - New Delhi - Hong Kong

First published in the UK by Scholastic Ltd, 2000
Copyright © Carlton Cards Ltd, 2000
ISBN 0 439 99843 3

All rights reserved
Printed in Italy
2 4 6 8 10 9 7 5 3 1

This book is sold subject to the condition that it shall not, by way of trade or otherwise, be lent, resold, hired out, or otherwise circulated without the publisher's prior consent in any form of binding or cover other than that in which it is published and without a similar condition, including this condition, being imposed upon the subsequent purchaser.

Come Hang With The Gang

Bubblegum is the first and last word in COOL. It's fab 'n' funky and it's got street cred by the bucket load. It's more fun than dancing with your mad nan and what's more, its nutty verse will make you laugh your socks off!

Inside you'll find out why Drama Queen makes a crisis out of every drama, why Cool Dude is soooo cool and which of the Bubblegum Crew is a proper flippin' babe magnet.

Put your feet up, have a cuppa and work out which of your mates is the archetypal Disco Diva, Choccy Fiend or Hunny Bunny La (ahhh!). Then flip to the back of the book and see who else you've spotted!

Go on – have fun, turn a few pages and enjoy reading about the grooviest crew in the universe!

When she gets glammed up for groovin'
she feels that funky fever
She's delicious and delightful
she's a diamond Disco Diva!

Disco Divas just don't care
they'll shake their thang just anywhere!

Disco Diva

'Gorgeously glitteringly glam' is the only way you can describe Disco Diva. She's a twenty-four hour party girl with an ear for a big boomin' seventies' anthem. She loves to dance around at home or to the stereo in Boy Racer's car. She'll jump in, turn the volume up on his stereo and declare "Disco Diva's in the house". She's a one-way ticket to the 'in-crowd' and people tend to worship the ground she dances on. Slightly dippy, but who cares when you're this gorgeous?

Most Likely to Say... Turn it up!

Most Likely to Be... On the dance floor

Fave Colour Candy Pink

Bestest Friends with... Nutty Tart, Sparkle Sista, Boy Racer

DISCO DIVA

Cool Dude

Cool Dude is the hippest bloke around. He's cooler than a penguin in a fridge and laid back to California. He is hip and very trendy. Trademark shades and goatee beard make this dude a distinctive purveyor of cool. He can be found sampling the jazz at the record store or drinking a cappuccino with friends in the 'Cafe Bub'– that's where Cool Street joins Happenin' Square. If you need advice on anything cool or trendy then Cool Dude is the bloke to see. If you need to be one of the 'in-crowd' then Cool Dude is the bloke to be seen with!

Most Likely to Say... Yeah, whatever!

Most Likely to Be... Listening to sounds or chillin' out in a cafe

Fave Colour Ice Blue

Bestest Friends with... Groovy Chick, Happenin' Babe, Easy

He's too damn smooth for anything
no time for sleep or food
He swans around just being him
the coolest ever dude.

At being cool he's really brill
'cos he's the master of how to chill.

You dream of swimming in it
and you never could be weaned
You're a chocolate-covered, sugar-smothered
mad, bad choccy fiend!

Choccy fiends love to munch
choccy for brekky, dinner and lunch!

Choccy Fiend

She's mad about all things chocolate! She even has a bar for her breakfast. All that sugar gives her tons of energy which she likes to burn off running around at one hundred miles an hour, nattering and gossiping with anyone who'll listen. She's a real live-wire, you could say, a proper fruit-and-nut case!

Most Likely to Say...
Want a bit of this scrummy bar?

Most Likely to Be...
In the shop buying choccy

Fave Colour
Chocolate brown (what else?)

Bestest Friends with...
Sofa Spud 
Chatterbox
Nutty Moo

CHOCCY FIEND

Groovy Chick

Groovy Chick is the original IT girl. To put it quite simply she is 'The Chick'. Everything about her says 'groovy'. She's a fun-loving, stylish babe who everyone adores. She passed all her exams at 'The Ministry Of Cool' with flying colours. Bright 'n' breezy, she leaves a trail of enthusiasm wherever she goes and always carries her trademark flower with her.

Most Likely to Say... Hello Sunshine!

Most Likely to Be... Anywhere that's fun

Fave Colour Sunshine Yellow

Bestest Friends with... Hippy Chick, Cool Dude,   Happenin' Babe

GROOVY CHICK

She's wild, she's hip and crazy
she makes other girls quite sick
She's fantastic and she's funky
she's a gorgeous, groovy chick!

Groovy Chick's a girl with power
'cos she carries a great big flower!

She's a proper gorgeous girlie
a chick with a big mad 'do
What makes her so bloomin' spesh
is she's so nice through and through.

Blonde Bombshell loves to shake her hair
and boys get weak-kneed everywhere!

Blonde Bombshell

Blonde Bombshell is a proper babe. She's 100 percent gorgeous and a real stunner. When she's in the room all the boys go weak at the knees. She tells them all not to be so daft and floats around being totally irresistible.

Most Likely to Say... Gorgeous, who me?

Most Likely to Be... Surrounded by weak-kneed boys

Fave Colour Beach Blonde

Bestest Friends with... Glamour Puss, Designer Diva,  IT Girl

BLONDE BOMBSHELL

Now you may call it strawberry blonde or maybe copper, but it's ginger. If you disagree, you're off your ginger nut!

Ginger Nuts just don't care they go ginger nuts anywhere!

Ginger Nut

Ginger Nut is the full on 'Ginner' of the crew, although he likes to refer to his hair as strawberry blonde. He's a proper lad and likes a laugh and a joke, mostly at the expense of the girls. He can often be seen with his dog, Rusty, who follows him everywhere. If there's a buzz around Happenin' Square, you can be certain that Ginger Nut is right at the centre of it.

Most Likely to Say...
Wot you staring at?

Most Likely to Be...
In a mischievous mood

Fave Colour
Ginger of course!

Bestest Friends with...
Footy Nut
Sparkle Sista

100% Bad

GINGER NUT

Veggie

Veggie loves animals so much that her pad is like an unofficial zoo. She cares for all animals, from hedgehogs to cats and dogs with three legs. She's very caring and hopes to be a vet one day. She's happiest when she's munching on a veggie burger or chomping a mega salad.

Most Likely to Say... Mine's a lentil!

Most Likely to Be... In town campaigning against fox hunting

Fave Colour Tree Green

Bestest Friends with... Hippy Chick

Ceefer Cat

Cool Dude

VEGGIE

Eating little animals
ain't her idea of fun
She'll just chill on plates of Trill
and lentils in a bun!

Veggies are so kind and gentle
they'll go bonkers for a lentil!

He's so laid back he's just like
the leaning Tower of Pisa
He really is a triffic guy
a truly Diamond Geezer!

Diamond Geezer is a godsend
someone to turn to when you need a friend.

Diamond Geezer

Diamond Geezer is a top bloke. He's 100 percent reliable and when a friend is in need, he is a friend indeed. He's got shoulders to laugh on, cry on and even flippin' sit on when you're having a mega laugh. If you want someone to be there for you, then look no further than this diamond of a bloke.

Most Likely to Say...
Do you need to talk?

Most Likely to Be...
Helping an old git across the road

Fave Colour
Diamond White

Bestest Friends with...
Sun Junkie
Footy Nut
Petrol Head

DIAMOND GEEZER

Top Chick

Top Chick is just that, a proper top chick. This gal (who is Groovy Chick's little sis) has a heart of gold and a smile as wide as Hippy Chick's flares. She's delightfully bubbly and brings laughter, sunshine and a bloomin' big balloon with her everywhere she goes!

Most Likely to Say... Hey Sis! Can I come too?

Most Likely to Be... Tagging on to Groovy Chick

Fave Colour Balloon Red

Bestest Friends with... Hunny Bunny, Dancing Queen, Shoe Queen

TOP CHICK

Whenever Top Chick is around
there's sunshine round the place
She's groovy and clever, she'll party forever
a gal who is totally ace!

Top Chick is number one
she just loves tons of fun!

You're a groovy little funkster
cooler than any other
All shout wow – check it out now
it's the Funk Soul Brother!

Funk Soul Brothers love their toons
over music they're flippin' loons!

Funk Soul Brother

He's the hippest trendiest dude around. He's into his sounds big time and can be found playing his toons all over Happenin' Square. He'll remix and remix 'til he gets just the right blend of funkiness into his toon.

If you want to be with the 'in-crowd', then make sure you find Funk Soul Brother 'cos without him, things just ain't happenin'.

Most Likely to Say... Check this out

Most Likely to Be... Behind his mixing desk

Fave Colour Block Rockin' Black

Bestest Friends with... 100% Bad, Easy, Glamour Puss

FUNK SOUL BROTHER

Groovy Gal

She's a proper groovy babe and has all the boys drooling over her luscious looks and cool style. She's into all things mystical and likes nothing better than an afternoon spent shopping in the local market for unusual things. She has a groove all of her own and although she's often imitated, she can never be copied.

Most Likely to Say... Gosh! That's so pretty!

Most Likely to Be... Shopping for trinkets

Fave Colour Purple

Bestest Friends with... Nutty Tart, Happenin' Babe, Nutty Moo

GROOVY GAL

Groovy Gal is so delish
she's a real honey it's true
She's got style, by the mile
and she's proper groovy too!

Groovy Gal is a dish delight
see her groove right
thru the night!

He's badder than the baddest thing
all crazy, wild and mad
He's kickin' and he's ragin'
he's one hundred percent bad!

He's the one full of 'tude
mean 'n' nasty, cute 'n rude.

100% Bad

100 Percent Bad is the bad boy that everybody loves to love. He's mean, moody and macho and struts his stuff with tons of attitude and style. Recognisable by his trademark 'Bad' designer gear, he's the bloke to have around when things get tough.

Most Likely to Say... What of it?

Most Likely to Be... Wherever the action is

Fave Colour Bad Ass Blue

Bestest Friends with... Ginger Nut, Happenin' Babe,   Funk Soul Brother

Smile

Smile is so happy that she just can't smile wide enough. She's got an infectious, beaming, smashing smile that spreads sunshine and love to everyone she meets. If you are feeling a bit down or a little blue, then trust Smile to come 'round and put a big beaming smasher back on your chops! She's a big ray of fabness!

Most Likely to Say...
Smile - it's the universal language!

Most Likely to Be...
Where the fun is

Fave Colour
Smiley Yellow

Bestest Friends with...
Everybody!

Some people think it's wads of cash
that make a life worthwhile
But what makes the world a better place
is a super, smashing smile!

Smiles are smashing and really great
so why not flash one to a mate?

SLAP HEAD

Bonce Wax

It's not fair that people chuckle
when you take off your cap
Just because you've got a head
that people want to slap!

Slapheads just don't seem to care
that they've got pink instead of hair!

Slap Head

Slap Head is just that, a proper chrome dome. However, what he lacks in hair, he makes up for in personality. He is always the one to give it 'large'. As an older member of the gang, he often gives advice to the crew. His advice is plentiful and what he says most often is, "Forget your troubles and party, party, party!"

Most Likely to Say... It's not a bald head, it's a solar panel for a party machine!

Most Likely to Be... Letting the disco lights bounce off his bonce

Fave Colour Skin Pink (like his head)

Bestest Friends with... Boy Racer, Nutty Tart, Footy Nut

SLAP HEAD

Dancing Queen

Dancing Queen just loves to dance, no matter where she is. This crazy, dancing chick will strut her stuff whenever she hears a banging tune. She's the queen of the dance floor and will dance around her bag all night. She loves to throw wild parties with lots of music, lots of dancing and lots of fun. If you feel like a boogie, then Dancing Queen is the girl to be with.

Most Likely to Say... Got any ABBA?

Most Likely to Be... Shaking her thang on the dance floor

Fave Colour Glam Gold

Bestest Friends with... Top Chick, Shoe Queen, Hunny Bunny

DANCING QUEEN

As she gets down and gets funky
she makes other groovers green
She's the master moving, gorgeous, grooving
prancing Dancing Queen!

Dancing Queen just loves to strut
shake and dance and wiggle her butt!

DESIGNER DIVA

As she goes hunting round the high street
she gets that label fever
She really loves the fashion scene
she's a cool Designer Diva!

Designer Diva is mentally unstable
when it comes to the latest label!

DoNKeY

MOSCHEAPO
£250

poochi
£190

Veristarchi

Issa Myacne

Designer Diva

Designer Diva is a label hog — there's no question about it. She loves to show off her latest purchases. She'll shop 'til she drops, then get up and shop some more. She loves wearing labels with big logos, so everyone can see who makes her clothes. For heavens sake, she's even got Gucci slippers!

Most Likely to Say...
I'll take them all!

Most Likely to Be...
Shopping in posh shops

Fave Colour
Whatever the new black is

Bestest Friends with...
Blonde Bombshell  
IT Girl
Glamour Puss

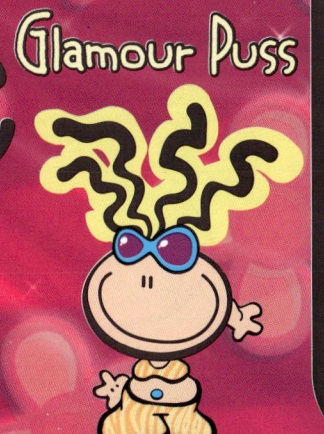

DESIGNER DIVA

Boy Racer

Boy Racer loves his car more than anything else. It's his pride and joy and he polishes it twice a day. It's a proper flippin' pose-mobile. He likes to cruise around with Groovy Chick and Disco Diva. When he's not in his car, he still dashes around at one hundred miles an hour. He lives life in the fast lane. Boy Racer by name, definitely Boy Racer by nature.

Most Likely to Say...
Do you like my wheels?

Most Likely to Be...
In the car shop buying polish

Fave Colour
Porsche Red

Bestest Friends with...
Disco Diva 
Footy Nut
Petrol Head

BOY RACER

As he goes screeching past the bus stop
I'm sure that every girl does vow
To get to touch his fluffy dice –
a real Boy Racer wow!

Boy Racer loves to ride and pose
wearing sunglasses on his nose.

She's got stacks and stacks of shoes
she's got a million different pairs
Piled high up in the wardrobe
or stuffed beneath the stairs.

Shoe Queen thinks it's really neat
to buy tons of shoes for her feet!

BIG SHOE SALE!

Shoos 'n' Wotnot

Shoe Queen

As her name suggests, Shoe Queen's biggest love is shoes. She has a billion pairs and wears the maddest, wackiest shoes you can imagine. When she's not buying shoes, she is wondering where to put the last lot she bought in the sale. She's got more pairs than a disco lovin' centipede!

Most Likely to Say... I must have those shoes!

Most Likely to Be... Trying on shoes!

Fave Colour Not bothered – as long as they have them in her size

Bestest Friends with... Hunny Bunny, Top Chick, Dizzy

SHOE QUEEN

Hunny Bunny

Ahhhh! She's the cutest of the Bubblegum Crew. She's everyone's little sister. Hunny Bunny doesn't say much, but what she says is as sweet as cherry pie. She's got a bloomin' big aura about her and is everyone's favourite cuddle.

Most Likely to Say... Hug Me

Most Likely to Be... In the sweet shop

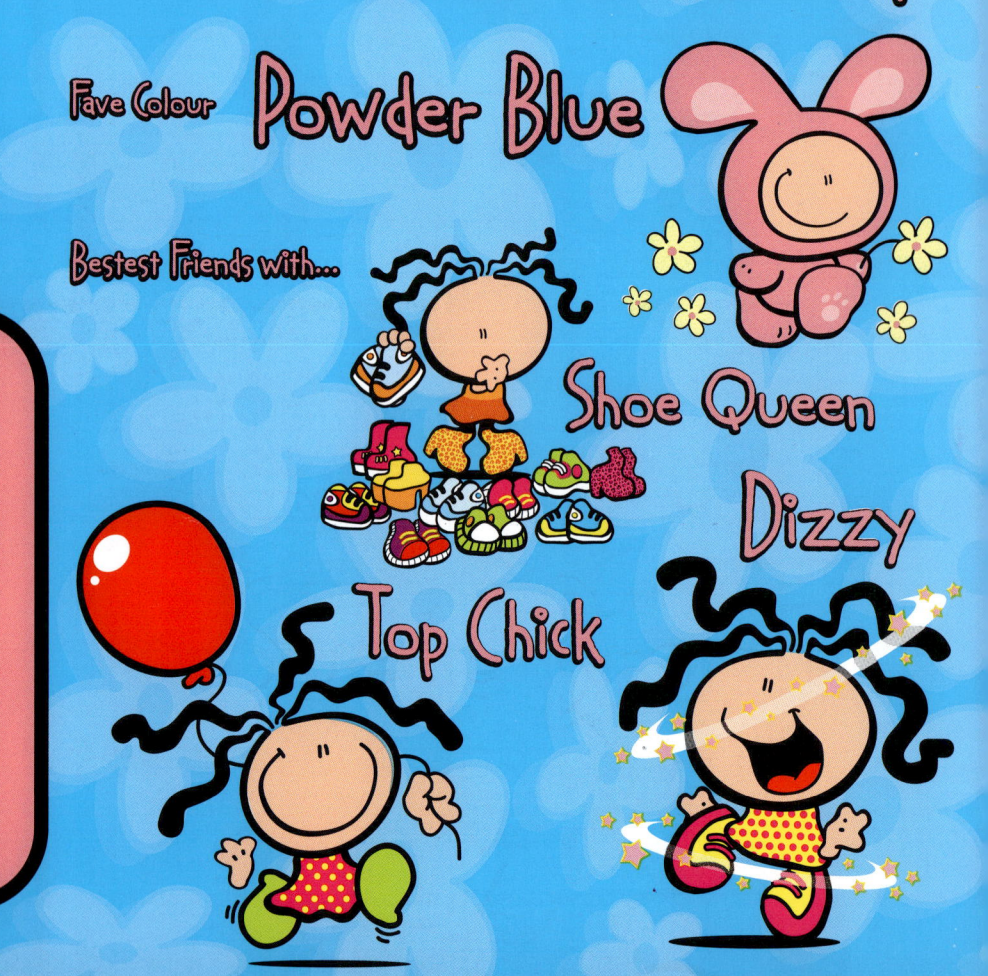

Fave Colour Powder Blue

Bestest Friends with... Shoe Queen, Top Chick, Dizzy

HUNNY BUNNY

She's lovely and she's gorgeous
she's mad, and oh, so funny
Always glad, she's never sad
an adorable Hunny Bunny!

Hunny Bunnies are so sweet
scrummy enough to flippin' eat!

Sweets

Boing ✤ Boin

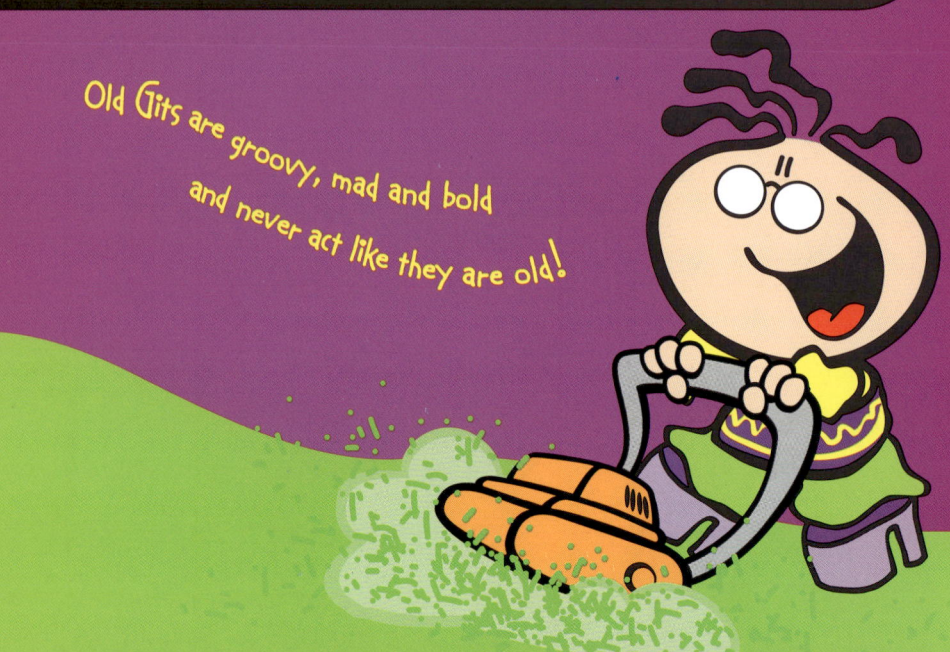

He remembers tank tops
his platform boots still fit
It's plain to see, as you'll agree
he's a proper nice Old Git!

Old Gits are groovy, mad and bold
and never act like they are old!

Old Git

Old Git is the oldest member of the Bubblegum Crew. You'll find him shaking his head at Disco Diva, and sighing loudly in the Post Office queue when he's standing behind a bopping Dancing Queen. Although he's ancient, all the crew love him to bits and he has been known to enjoy himself!

Most Likely to Say...

In the eighties, things were different...

Most Likely to Be...

Doing the garden or something ancient like that

Fave Colour

Brown

Bestest Friends with...

Football Crazy

Groovy Gran

Deefer Dog

OLD GIT

Sun Junkie

As her name suggests, Sun Junkie loves the sunshine. She's forever in a teeny weeny bikini and she likes to soak up the rays whenever she can. Consequently she thinks life's a beach and loves nothing better than a beach party and a frolic in the sea.

Most Likely to Say... Is it sunny out today?

Most Likely to Be... Soaking up the rays on the beach

Fave Colour Golden Brown

Bestest Friends with... Blonde Bombshell, Glamour Puss, Smile

SUN JUNKIE

She's always soaking up the rays
she looks so tanned and funky
On the beach she lies on her towel
a nicely browned Sun Junkie!

Sun Junkies spend their days
lying back and catching rays.

She's not all quiet, reserved and shy
'cos that just wouldn't do
She's monsterly scatty, crazy and batty
the nuttiest ever Moo!

Nutty Moos are as mad as cheese
'cos everyone they love to tease!

Toot Toot

Toot Toot

Nutty Moo

Nutty Moo is just that – an absolutely nutty chick with heaps of personality. She's a larger-than-life gal who is always fooling around, pulling faces and having the largest of laughs. She never takes anything seriously and will gladly laugh her way through the day, blowing big wet raspberries at her troubles.

Most Likely to Say... Who cares?

Most Likely to Be... Pulling a daft face at the world

Fave Colour Friesian

Bestest Friends with... Choccy Fiend, Crazy Lady, Groovy Gal

NUTTY MOO

Chatterbox

Chatterbox loves to natter, natter, natter. She never shuts up and will talk about anything for hours and hours and hours. She's never off the telephone and loves to catch up on all the latest gossip with her friends. She bends everybody's ears with her constant nattering, but everybody loves her because with Chatterbox there's never a dull (or a quiet) moment.

Most Likely to Say... Have you heard what happened to...

Most Likely to Be... On the phone or gossiping in Café Bub

Fave Colour Yapping Yellow

Bestest Friends with...

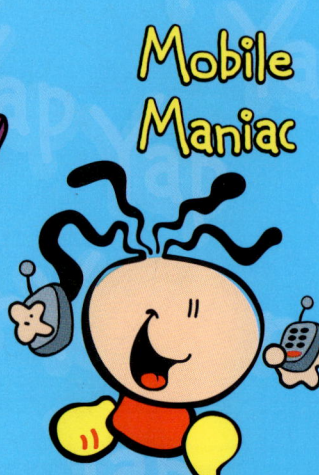

Nutty Tart

Choccy Fiend

Mobile Maniac

CHATTERBOX

To keep her quiet you can try
to stuff her face with chocs,
But nothing ever seems to work
she's a chitter, chatterbox!

Chatterboxes love to natter
you hear them coming by their chatter.

HAPPENIN' BABE   HAPPENIN' BABE   HAPPENIN' BABE

You know the score and where it's at
you're on a one-way trendiness trip
You're in the groove, you're too damn smooth
a babe that's happenin' 'n' hip!

She's the bestest coolest cat
Happenin' Babe is where it's at!

Happenin' Babe

She's the babe who really knows where it's at. She's hip, she's happenin' and she's totally cool. She drives around in her Beetle convertible looking all sophisticated. If you're looking for a trendsetter or want to know what to wear for the coming season, just ask Happenin' Babe and she'll be only too pleased to put you straight.

Most Likely to Say... It's so gorgeous!

Most Likely to Be... Where it's happenin'

Fave Colour Jade Green

Bestest Friends with... Groovy Chick   Groovy Gal

100% Bad

HAPPENIN' BABE

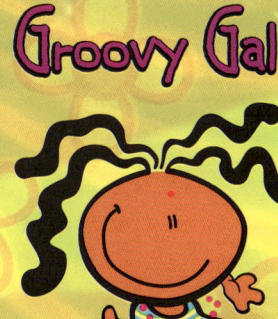

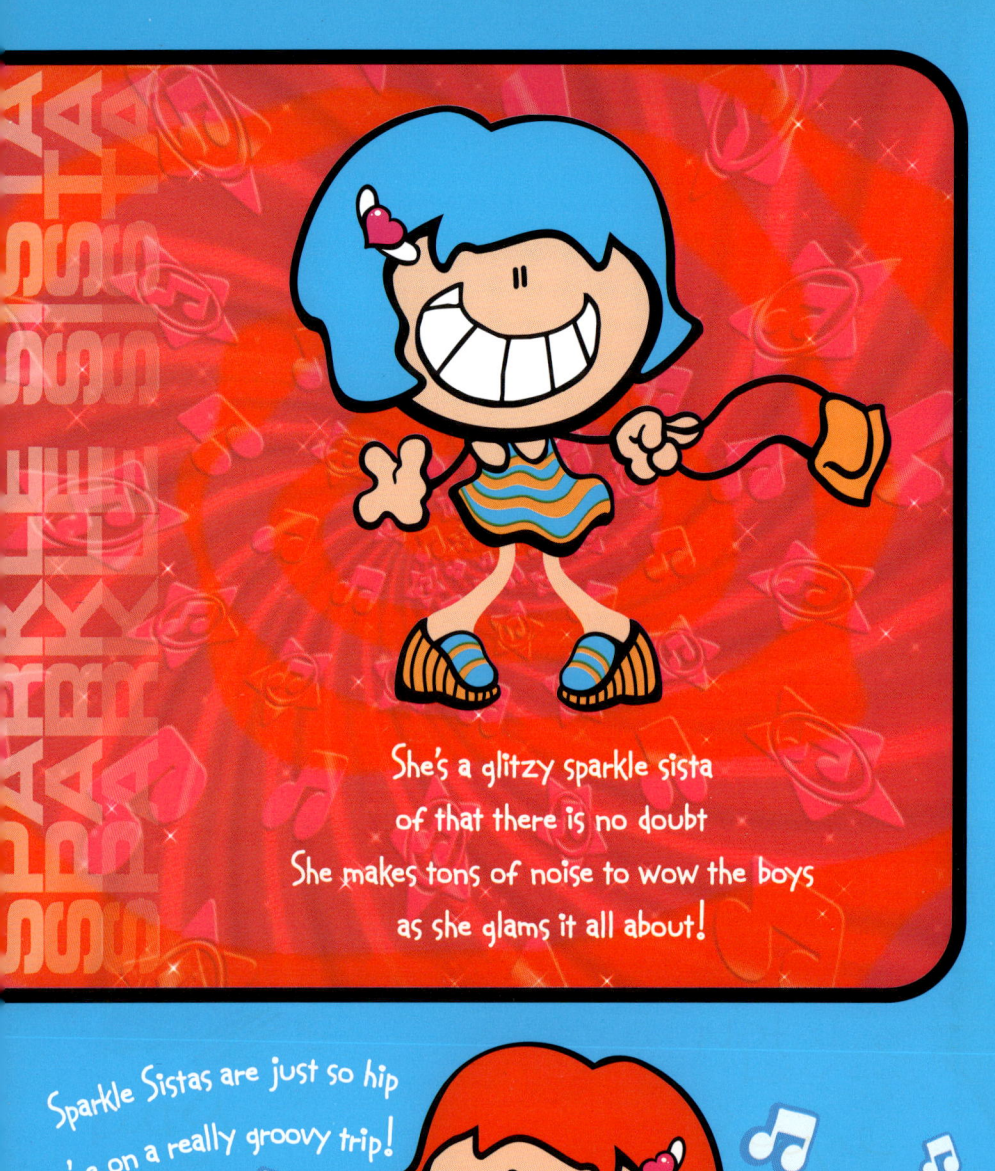

She's a glitzy sparkle sista
of that there is no doubt
She makes tons of noise to wow the boys
as she glams it all about!

Sparkle Sistas are just so hip
they're on a really groovy trip!

Sparkle Sista

She's the style sista with the blue hair and the infectious laugh. She's a proper funky monkey, a girl full of fun. Everyone wishes they had a best friend just like her. She's way out on her own when it comes to individual style and class. She's got the maddest hair you've ever seen – most of the time it's blue, but like Sparkle Sista it can change on a whim. Two words for this coolest of chicks, 'She sparkles'.

Most Likely to Say... Look at me!

Most Likely to Be... The centre of attention

Fave Colour Electric Blue

Bestest Friends with... Ginger Nut, Dancing Queen, Disco Diva

SPARKLE SISTA

Nutty Tart

Nutty Tart's nuttier than a squirrel's supper. She is the craziest of the Bubblegum Crew and always bounces around having a truly nutty time. Wild, wacky and wonderful, she makes any gathering complete (completely mad that is!).

Most Likely to Say... Have a 'narna!

Most Likely to Be... Out to lunch

Fave Colour Sea Green

Bestest Friends with...

Disco Diva

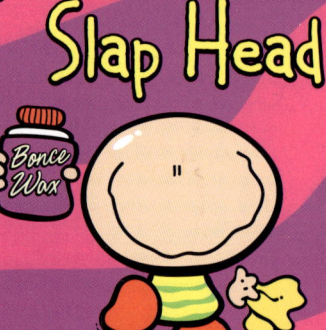

Groovy Gal

Slap Head

NUTTY TART

She's crazy and she's scatty
a real class apart
It's fair to say in every way
she's a grade 'A' nutty tart!

Nutty Tart is just plain nutty
nuttier than a squirrel's butty!

Line Dancer

Yeeeeehhhhahh! Line Dancer is a serious line dancing fan. She can be seen dressed up as a cowgirl on a Wednesday night, heading for the local village hall. There she will dance in a big soft line to 'Achy Breaky Heart' with other like-minded cowgirls and boys.

Most Likely to Say...
Don't break my achy breaky heart

Most Likely to Be...
In a draughty church hall, in a line, in some mad cowgirl gear!

Fave Colour
Suede Brown

Bestest Friends with...
Dancing Queen
Mex Tex

LINE DANCER